RAMADAN
AND ID-UL-FITR

FESTIVALS AND **FAITHS**

RAMADAN
AND ID-UL-FITR

ROSALIND KERVEN

Evans

First published in this edition in 2010 by
Evans Brothers Limited
2A Portman Mansions
Chiltern Street
London W1U 6NR

British Library Cataloguing in Publication Data
Kerven, Rosalind.
        Ramadan and Id-ul-Fitr. -- (Festivals and
faiths)
        1. Id al-Fitr--Juvenile literature. 2. Ramadan--
        Juvenile literature.
        I. Title II. Series
        394.2'657-dc22

ISBN 978 0 237 54123 1

Printed in China

ACKNOWLEDGEMENTS

Editor: Su Swallow
Design: Neil Sayer
Production: Jenny Mulvanny

The author and publishers would like to thank the
Muslim Educational Trust for their help in the
preparation of this book.

The author and publishers would like to think the
following for permission to reproduce photographs:

Cover: (top) Axiom/Jim Holmes, (bottom and
back) Trip

page 6 Trip page 7 (top and bottom) Trip page 8
Sarah Errington, Hutchison Library page 9 Trip
page 10 Circa Photo Library page 11 Axiom/Jim
Holmes page 12 Axiom/Jim Holmes page 13 Trip
page 14 Circa Photo Library page 15 (top) Carlos
Freire, Hutchison Library (bottom) Trip page 16
John Miles/Panos Pictures page 17 Trip page 18 Trip
page 19 Trip page 20 Trip page 21 Circa Photo
Library page 22 Trip page 23 (top and bottom) Trip
page 24 Trip page 25 Trip page 26 Circa Photo
Library page 27 (top and bottom) Trip

Contents

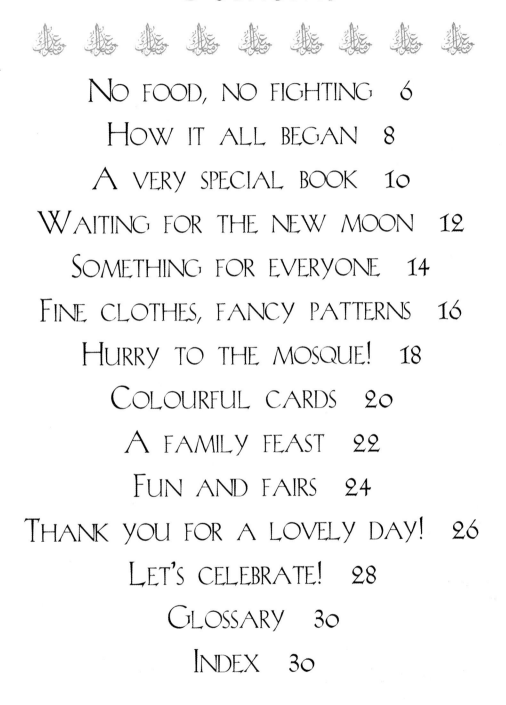

No food, no fighting 6

How it all began 8

A very special book 10

Waiting for the new moon 12

Something for everyone 14

Fine clothes, fancy patterns 16

Hurry to the mosque! 18

Colourful cards 20

A family feast 22

Fun and fairs 24

Thank you for a lovely day! 26

Let's celebrate! 28

Glossary 30

Index 30

No food, no fighting

WAKE UP! The new day is breaking and a bright lamp is burning in the minaret of the local mosque. It's the first day of Ramadan, the Muslim holy month, when most adults, and many older children, 'fast' (go without any food or drink) from dawn until sunset.

Everyone has an early breakfast. Then gradually the sky gets lighter. The Qur'an (the Muslim holy book) says that fasting must begin when it is light enough to tell the difference between a white thread and a black one.

A TIME TO THINK

Fasting is quite difficult and uncomfortable, but it reminds Muslims how lucky they are to have enough to eat and drink the rest of the time. It makes them think of the world's poor people who never have enough food or clean water.

This restaurant in Tunisia is closed every day during Ramadan.

Whenever they feel hungry or thirsty during Ramadan, Muslims try to think of good deeds they could do to say 'thank you' to God for all the happy things in life.

EVERYONE'S TOGETHER

In a Muslim community or country, everyone fasts together during Ramadan, which helps to make a good feeling of friendliness. They also try not to argue or be angry during Ramadan.

As the sun sets, it's time for *iftar*, the evening meal. This usually starts with something light, such as dates or apricots soaked in sweetened water, or perhaps a special drink of sweetened, spicy milk. After that, everyone can eat and drink as much as they need during the hours of darkness.

Ramadan cakes on sale

The evening meal tastes especially good after a day of fasting!

 How it all began

ABOUT 1,400 YEARS AGO, a man called Muhammad lived in the city of Makkah (now in modern Saudi Arabia). He became the Prophet of God. During Ramadan young Muslims often listen to this story of his life.

Muslim children in Kyrgystan, in Central Asia, reading the Qur'an. Like all Muslim children, they learn to read the Qur'an in Arabic, even though Arabic is not their own language.

THE FIRST MUSLIMS

Muhammad was very upset by all the poverty, cruelty and violence he saw in the world. To escape from it, he used to go off into the desert on his own for long periods, to think.

One day while he was alone in a desert cave, he suddenly saw a vision of the Angel Jibril (Gabriel) and heard a voice saying,

'Recite! In the name of thy Lord who has created everything, who has created Man from a clot of blood.'

At first, Muhammad was frightened. He went home and talked about this vision with his wife, Khadijah. With her support, he soon realised that it really was a direct message from God.

Muhammad received many more messages through the Angel Jibril over the next 23 years. Many were about God. They also explained all the rules for living a good life.

Soon Muhammad began to obey the angel's command to 'recite'. He started to repeat these messages to other people, who became his followers. They were the first Muslims, Muhammad was their Prophet, and this was how the religion of Islam began.

Muslims come from all over the world to pray in the grand mosque in Makkah. They all face the Ka'bah, the stone monument in the middle.

9

A very special book

L IKE MOST PEOPLE OF his time, Muhammad could not read or write, but his messages were carefully remembered and repeated by special

Copies of the Qur'an are often beautifully decorated, to show that it is a very special, holy book.

'reciters'. They were written down about twenty years after his death, to form the Qur'an. This holy book has 114 chapters and more than 6,000 verses.

PRECIOUS AND BEAUTIFUL

The Qur'an is usually kept carefully wrapped up in a safe place. When someone reads aloud from it, everyone listens quietly.

The Qur'an is written in Arabic. This is the language that Muhammad spoke. The Qur'an has been translated into most of the world's different languages, but Muslims in every country still try to learn it off by heart in Arabic.

THE FIVE PILLARS

Muslims try very hard to live by the rules laid down in the Qur'an. They believe that God made these rules to show people how to live happily together. The most important rules are known as the 'Five Pillars' of Islam. One of these is fasting during Ramadan. The others are: belief in God; regular prayer; giving to charity; and making a pilgrimage to the holy city of Makkah.

Arabic script on the wall of a mosque.

A girl in Pakistan uses a special bookrest to hold the Qur'an.

Waiting for the new moon

Muslim women shopping, in preparation for the festivities to come.

MUSLIMS HAVE THEIR OWN SPECIAL CALENDAR. It is a 'lunar' calendar, based on the cycles of the moon. The Muslim year is about 11 days shorter than in Western (modern) calendars.

So the exact date of Ramadan changes every year. In 2009 it started on 21 August. In 2015 it will probably begin on 18 June.

WATCHING AND WAITING

By the 29th day of Ramadan everyone is wondering when the new moon will appear in the sky. This will signal the complete end of fasting, and the start of a very happy festival. In some years the moon does not appear until the 30th day, which means a whole extra day of fasting!

On the last night, many people stay up late for hours, excitedly watching and waiting for the moon. This can be very frustrating in countries where the weather is often bad, because sometimes the whole sky is covered by cloud. To get round this, Muslim leaders in Europe and the USA might telephone their friends living in hotter countries to ask whether the moon has been spotted there.

At last - there it is! The hardship of Ramadan has been successfully completed. Now it is the first day of the new month, Shawwal, and time to celebrate the festival of Id-ul-Fitr. In countries where most people are Muslims, this usually marks the beginning of an official public holiday, with no school or work for at least two days.

The moon above a mosque in Dubai, in the United Arab Emirates. When the new moon appears, Ramadan will be over, and the happy festival of Id-ul-Fitr can begin.

13

Something for everyone

As Ramadan comes to an end, everyone makes a special small payment to charity, known as *Zakat-ul-Fitr*. This is usually the amount of money needed to buy a meal for each person in the family. It is collected together and given to a charity. The charity uses the money to prepare food for poor Muslims who cannot afford enough food to enjoy Id-ul-Fitr.

Happy to pay

As well as this special collection, many Muslims pay another type of *zakat* once a year, every year. It is used to help the poor and needy. Islam teaches that everyone is equal in God's eyes, so that rich people should help poor people. Paying *zakat* is one of the Five Pillars of Islam. It is an important duty, and everyone is happy to pay it. There are special rules for calculating how much each person should pay, depending on how rich they are.

Zakat helps people who cannot earn enough money for themselves. It is also used for homeless people, orphans, prisoners, travellers in need, and people who are studying Islam. Nobody feels too proud or ashamed to receive it, for the Qur'an teaches that all wealth really belongs to God anyway, so it should be shared out fairly.

Muslims are always very happy to give zakat. The money collected goes to help other Muslims who are poor and in need.

Zakat may be used to help people who are studying Islam. These children are learning the Qur'an in India.

Old Islamic coins

Fine clothes, fancy patterns

ON THE MORNING OF ID-UL-FITR, the whole family gets up early. Everyone has a bath or shower, and then dresses up in their best clothes. The luckiest ones have brand new clothes specially for Id!

Many Muslims follow careful religious rules when choosing what to wear. They select long, loose, simple clothes, and women often wear a scarf over their hair. Islam teaches that women and girls should cover their whole bodies apart from the face and hands, whilst men and boys must be covered at least between the waist and the knees. Some people manage to fit these rules very well into the fashions of their country.

ALL THE TRIMMINGS

A special perfume is often worn by both women and men at Id. This tradition was started by the prophet Muhammad, who founded the Muslim religion (see pages 8 and 9).

Girls and women often decorate their hands with reddish-brown *mehndi* patterns. These might look like trailing flowers and leaves, or

simply twirling, abstract shapes. The colour is made from dried henna leaves, which are ground up into a powder, mixed with a little lemon juice and water, and then painted on with a matchstick or toothpick.

When everyone is ready, it's time for early morning prayers, and then a light breakfast snack, perhaps of sweets and dates.

On special occasions, such as weddings and festivals, women paint patterns on their hands.

Muslims wear their best clothes for Id. Like most Muslim women and girls, this girl is careful to cover her hair.

Hurry to the mosque!

AFTER BREAKFAST it is time to go out to the mosque (the Muslim place of worship). There is always an enormous crowd there at Id. In some places there are so many people that the service overflows outside the main building. In hot countries, Id prayers may be specially held in a large park or even a field.

Inside a busy mosque at Id in Cairo, Egypt.

As everyone hurries through the streets, they can hear the muezzin calling them. He stands in the minaret (tower) of the mosque crying in Arabic, 'God is the greatest! ... Come to prayer!'. He might use a loudspeaker to make sure he can be heard a long way off.

As they enter the mosque, each person stops to wash in the special washroom, or at the fountain. Then they go into the prayer-hall, the women and girls using a separate area from the men and boys. There are no chairs or seats in there, but the walls may be beautifully decorated with patterns and Arabic calligraphy (writing).

PRAYERS AND PEACE

At last the muezzin calls out, ' Prayer is ready!'. The imam (prayer leader) takes his place in the minbar (pulpit) and the service begins. Everyone joins in special Id prayers to say 'thank you' to God, and to ask for help to live a good life and obey all the laws of Islam. After prayers are

A mosque in Uzbekistan, in Central Asia is overflowing with worshippers, so some people have to pray outside.

finished, each person turns toward their neighbours saying 'Salaam' ('Peace be on you'). Then they listen as the imam gives a special talk, perhaps about helping other people through charity. Muslims always try to celebrate festivals in a way that will please God.

Then everyone comes spilling out of the mosque to greet their relations and friends. There are lots of happy smiles and hugs! The children are especially excited as they admire each other's new clothes.

Colourful cards

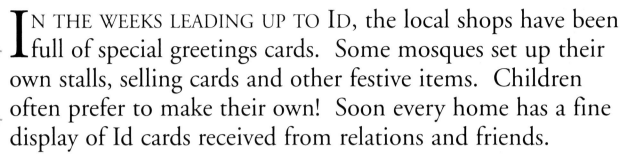

IN THE WEEKS LEADING UP TO ID, the local shops have been full of special greetings cards. Some mosques set up their own stalls, selling cards and other festive items. Children often prefer to make their own! Soon every home has a fine display of Id cards received from relations and friends.

PATTERNS, NOT PICTURES

The front of an Id card usually has a beautiful pattern of flowers, leaves, vines, stars or intricate shapes and twirling lines. Sometimes they might show a garden, a mosque, a pattern of decorated arches, or a design of stars and the moon. However, you will never see pictures of people or animals on an Id card. This is because Muslims believe that if an artist draws or paints a living creature, he or she will be punished for trying to copy God's unique powers of creation.

Children at a London mosque proudly display their home-made Id cards.

WRITING AS ART

Id cards are often brightly coloured. Blue and gold are especially popular: they symbolise Heaven and the sun.

Inside the card there is usually a special greeting, such as 'Best wishes for the Happy Id' or 'Wishing you the blessings of Id'. This is often witten in Arabic, followed by English or another local language.

Arabic has a completely different alphabet from English. It is written from right to left, so that Id cards are folded on the righthand side. The Arabic message is often written in beautiful, sweeping strokes.

Decorated
Id cards

A family feast

AFTER THEY LEAVE THE MOSQUE, many people go visiting their relations. Relations in the 'extended family' (grandparents, uncles, aunts and cousins) are very important to most Muslims. Muslim children are taught to treat all their relations with respect, especially elderly people such as their grandparents. At Id, all the family get together to celebrate, eat and have fun.

'HOPE YOU'RE HUNGRY!'

As the visitors arrive at their relations' house, people call out *'Id Mubarak!'* ('Happy festival!'). They often bring presents, such as gift-wrapped packs of sweets or dried fruits such as apricots, figs or sultanas, and money for the children.

Around midday, the whole family sits down to enjoy a special Id meal.

These children have been given a sweet for Id.

EAT WELL

Muslims try to prepare their best dishes for their guests on Id day. Mostly it is the women who do the cooking, but some men like to help in the kitchen on Id day. There is no special food for Id – it depends on where the people live. In India, Muslims might eat a delicious Id pudding made of rice or fine pasta. It is sweet and spicy and quite filling. Muslims do not eat pork, but they eat other meat, which has to be killed in a special way. They do not drink alcohol. On festival days they like to drink something sweet and refreshing.

Some people have lots of houses to visit at Id – and they will be given something to eat at each one!

A stall selling dried fruits in Morocco. People give dried fruits as presents at Id.

Eating is an important part of Id celebrations.

Fun and fairs

AFTER THE MEAL IS OVER, there is often a party for the 'extended family'. In some Muslim countries there are special fairs, parades and entertainments.

Id is a good time for family outings. Some people like to visit famous buildings or watch dancers and listen to music. The performers might dress up in their national costume.

Other people make their own music, and join in the dancing. Children like to try out all the rides at the funfair.

The paintings of Id are by Muslim children. The painting above shows an Id fair in Turkey. The painting on the left shows men dancing with swords to drum music.

▶ Dancing in the park in Cairo, in Egypt, during Id

Thank you for a lovely day!

IT'S BEEN A VERY LONG, exciting and happy day, and now it's time to go to bed. But good Muslim children, like their parents, would not dream of doing this until they have said their prayers.

A father and son pray at home

Muslims pray five times a day. The first prayers are said before sunrise. The other prayer times are: midday, mid-afternoon, after sunset, and before bedtime. Because they pray so often, Muslims never forget the importance of God in their lives.

AN EVERYDAY CEREMONY

The best place to pray is in a mosque, but of course, this is not possible for most people, most of the time. So Muslims are used to praying at home, at school, at work - or wherever they happen to be.

A prayer compass showing which way to face to pray

Before praying, Muslims always have a good wash. Then they turn to face the holy city of Makkah (see pages 9 and 10). Many people have a special compass to show the right direction.

BEAUTIFUL MATS

Muslims pray using special movements. They stand, hold up their hands, cross them over the waist, bow, then kneel and touch the floor with their nose and forehead.

Praying in a mosque. Even young children say their prayers five times a day.

Because they have to kneel and touch the floor, most people roll out prayer mats to make it more comfortable. These are often decorated with Islamic patterns. Some people are lucky enough to have really beautiful, thickly woven prayer mats.

SPECIAL THOUGHTS

After saying the set prayers in Arabic, people usually add a special private prayer of their own, in their own language. You can guess what most children will be adding tonight - they'll be saying thank you for all the lovely food, presents and fun they've had this Id-ul-Fitr.

Many people own beautifully decorated prayer mats.

27

Let's celebrate!

MAKE AN ID PUDDING

You will need:

    measuring cup
    teaspoon
    large spoon for stirring
    saucepan
    serving dish ($\frac{1}{2}$-litre size)
    2 cups of vermicelli,
       broken into small pieces.
    $\frac{1}{2}$ cup of margarine
    2 cups water
    $\frac{1}{4}$ cup sugar
    $\frac{1}{4}$ cup raisins
    $\frac{1}{4}$ cup flaked almonds
    $\frac{1}{4}$ teaspoon vanilla essence
    2 glacé cherries (cut in half)

Ask an adult to help you.

1. Wash your hands.
2. Put the broken vermicelli into the saucepan with the water.
3. Bring it to the boil, then turn the heat down.
4. Stir the vermicelli occasionally to stop it sticking to the pan.
5. Continue cooking on a low heat until all the water has evaporated (about 8 minutes).
6. Remove the saucepan from the heat.
7. Add margarine, sugar, vanilla essence, almonds and raisins to the vermicelli.
8. Stir until the margarine has melted and all the ingredients are well mixed.
9. Turn into the serving dish.
10. Smooth the top and decorate with glacé cherries.

MAKE AN ID CARD

You will need:

> one sheet of stiff paper or card
> paints, coloured pencils or felt-tip pens

1. Fold the card. Remember to keep the fold on the righthand side!

2. Choose one of these ideas to draw:

> flowers and leaves
> a garden
> stars and the moon
> a mosque or part of a mosque

3. Draw it on the front of the card. (Do not draw any animals, birds or people.)

4. Colour it in brightly. Try to make it look really beautiful.

5. Copy out this piece of Arabic writing inside, on the lefthand side.

6. Underneath write 'Best wishes for the Happy Id'. Try to make your writing really beautiful and decorated.

Glossary

Arabic – the language spoken in Arabia, much of North Africa and the Middle East. Also the holy language of Islam

calligraphy – beautiful handwriting

charity – giving money to those in need

community – a group of people

fast, fasting – going without food for religious reasons

imam – Muslim prayer leader

Islam – the Muslim religion

mosque – Muslim place of worship

muezzin – Muslim who calls people to prayer at the mosque

Muslim – someone who believes in the religion of Islam

Prophet – a special religious teacher who explains God's will to the people

Qur'an – the holy book of Islam.

Index

Angel Jibril 9
Arabic 8, 10, 11, 21
art 20, 21, 24

calendar 12
cards 20, 21, 29
charity 14
clothes 16, 17

family 22, 24
fasting 6, 7
Five Pillars 10, 14
food 7, 14, 22, 23, 28

God 8, 9, 10, 14, 26

Id-ul-Fitr 12-29
iftar 7
imam 18

Ka'bah 9

Makkah 8, 9, 10, 26
mehndi 16
minbar 18
mosque 11, 13, 18, 19
muezzin 18
Muhammad 8, 9, 10, 16

pilgrimage 10
prayer 18, 26, 27

Qur'an 6, 10, 11, 14, 15

Ramadan 6, 7, 10, 12

Shawwal 12

zakat 14
Zakat-ul-Fitr 14